AMERICA HATES HISTORY

Parker Voss

The paradox of why Americans hate history, but love nostalgia is one that has puzzled scholars and historians for years. This contradiction can be seen across all aspects of American society, including literature, film, and popular culture. While Americans may hate to study history in school, they often have a deep fascination with the past, particularly the nostalgic aspects of it. In this essay, we will explore this paradox by examining the historical context of the 1880s and relevant examples illustrate the American love of nostalgia.

Table of Contents

1880's

In the 1880s, America was undergoing significant social, economic, and political changes. It was a time of industrialization and urbanization, with the growth of cities and the rise of big business. This period marked the beginning of the Gilded Age, a time of rapid economic growth but also rampant corruption and social inequality.

One of the most significant events of the 1880s was the rise of the dime novel. Dime novels were cheap, sensationalistic books were sold for ten cents or less. They were a form of popular entertainment featuring sensational stories about cowboys, detectives, and other larger-than-life characters. Dime novels were immensely popular during the 1880s, and they helped to create the myth of the American West. These stories often glorified the frontier and presented a romanticized version of the cowboy hero. They also helped to perpetuate the idea of the Wild West as a lawless and violent place, which further fueled Americans' fascination with the past.

Another significant event of the 1880s was the construction of the Statue of Liberty. The statue was a gift from France to America, and it symbolized the friendship between the two countries. It was also a symbol of American freedom and democracy, and it quickly became an icon of American culture. The statue was completed in 1886, and it was dedicated by President Grover Cleveland in a ceremony that attracted thousands of people. The statue helped to create a sense of national pride and identity, and it became a popular tourist attraction.

Despite the significant changes happening in America during the 1880s, many Americans felt a sense of nostalgia. This nostalgia was often expressed through literature, music, and art. For example, the popular song "After the Ball" was written in 1891, but it reflected a sense of nostalgia. The song tells the story of a man who regrets not telling a woman he loved her when he had the chance. The lyrics are sentimental and wistful, and they reflect a longing for a simpler time.

Another example of the American love of nostalgia during the 1880s is the popularity of the Arts and Crafts movement. The Arts and Crafts movement was a reaction against the industrialization of America and the loss of traditional crafts and skills. It emphasized the importance of handcrafted goods and the beauty of nature. The movement was influenced by the writings of John Ruskin and William Morris, who believed industrialization was destroying the soul of the country. The Arts and Crafts movement helped to create a sense of nostalgia and the values were being lost in the modern world.

The paradox of why Americans hate history, but love nostalgia can be seen throughout American society. The

1880s were a time of momentous change in America, with the rise of industrialization, urbanization, and big business. However, Americans also had a deep fascination with the past, particularly the nostalgic aspects of it. The rise of the dime novel, the construction of the Statue of Liberty, and the popularity of the Arts and Crafts movement are all examples of the American love of nostalgia during the 1880s.

Americans' fascination with the past reflects a desire to understand their own identity and to connect with a simpler, more innocent time.

1890's

The 1890s were a decade of rapid change and development in the United States. It was a time when the country was transitioning from an agricultural society to an industrial one. During this decade, the population of the country increased by almost 13 million people (about twice the population of Arizona), and new inventions and technologies such as the automobile, telephone, and electric power transformed daily life.

Despite these changes, there is a paradoxical relationship between Americans and history during the 1890s. Many Americans expressed a deep-seated hatred of history, often viewing it as a dry, boring subject. At the same time, however, they were fascinated by nostalgia and romanticized visions of the past.

One example of this paradox can be seen in the popularity of cowboy stories and Wild West shows during the 1890s. At this time, many Americans were moving from rural areas to urban centers, leaving behind the lifestyle of the American West. However, the Wild West shows, and cowboy stories provided a romanticized and nostalgic version of the West, and Americans eagerly consumed them.

The popularity of the Wild West shows was due in part to the myth of the cowboy as a rugged individualist and hero. This image of the cowboy was popularized by dime novels and newspapers, and it became even more widespread with the advent of Buffalo Bill's Wild West show, which toured the country and even Europe. The show featured reenactments of famous events and characters from the American West, and it was wildly popular.

The popularity of the Wild West shows, and cowboy stories can also be seen in the popularity of the dime novel. These cheaply produced books featured stories of cowboys, Indians, and other Western characters, and they were extremely popular among young people. The dime novels were criticized by some for their sensational and unrealistic portrayal of the West, but they nevertheless provided a romanticized version of the past many Americans found appealing.

Another example of the paradox of hating history but loving nostalgia can be seen in the fascination with the Civil War during the 1890s. This was the 25th anniversary of the end of the war, and there was a renewed interest in the conflict. However, this interest was often focused on the heroism and bravery of the soldiers rather than on the complex causes and consequences of the war.

One example of this focus on heroism and bravery can be seen in the popularity of the Grand Army of the Republic (GAR), a fraternal organization made up of Union veterans of the Civil War. The organization was founded in 1866, but it reached the height of its popularity during the 1890s. The GAR held annual national encampments, which were attended by thousands of veterans and their families. These events included parades, speeches, and other activities that celebrated the heroism and sacrifice of the soldiers.

The fascination with the Civil War during the 1890s can also be seen in the popularity of monuments and memorials. Many towns and cities erected monuments to honor the soldiers who had fought and died in the war. These monuments often emphasized the heroism and bravery of the soldiers, and they were seen as a way of preserving the memory of the conflict.

Overall, the paradox of hating history but loving nostalgia can be seen throughout American history, and the 1890s were no exception. Americans during this decade were fascinated by romanticized versions of the past, whether it was the Wild West or the heroism of the Civil War soldiers. While they may have expressed a disdain for history as a subject, they nevertheless found meaning and inspiration in the past, even if it was a distorted version of it.

1900's

The early 1900s marked a turning point in American history. As the country continued to expand and industrialize, the nation's culture and values were rapidly changing. While some were excited about the changes, others were nostalgic for a simpler, more traditional way of life. This paradox of loving nostalgia while hating history is a recurring theme throughout American history and can be seen clearly in the early 1900s.

One example of this paradox is the popularity of the "Old Country" theme in American culture during the early 1900s. Many Americans had recently immigrated to the United States, bringing with them traditions and values from their home countries. These traditions were often romanticized and idealized, serving as a form of nostalgia for a simpler time and way of life. This nostalgia was evident in literature, art, and even architecture, as people sought to recreate the quaint, picturesque villages of Europe in their own communities.

At the same time, however, there was a widespread rejection of traditional history and culture. Many Americans viewed the old ways as outdated and backwards, preferring to embrace modern, progressive values. This rejection of tradition was evident in the widespread popularity of the "New Woman" movement, which advocated for women's rights and challenged traditional gender roles. The rise of industrialization and consumerism also fueled a rejection of the past, as people focused on the future and what was new and innovative.

Another example of this paradox is the nostalgia for the Wild West during the early 1900s. The American West had been romanticized in literature and film for decades, with cowboys, gunfights, and rugged individualism serving as symbols of American culture. This nostalgia was evident in the popularity of Wild West shows and rodeos, as well as the creation of Western-themed tourist attractions like ghost towns and dude ranches.

However, this nostalgia for the Wild West was also accompanied by a rejection of the actual history of the American West. The brutal treatment of Native Americans and the displacement of their communities was often ignored or downplayed in favor of a more heroic narrative of Western expansion. The real, complex history of the West was replaced by a simplified, nostalgic version played into American fantasies of rugged individualism and manifest destiny.

Finally, the early 1900s saw a growing interest in the preservation of historic sites and landmarks. Many Americans recognized the importance of preserving their country's history and heritage, leading to the establishment of national parks, monuments, and historic sites. However, this interest in history was often selective and superficial. Many historic sites were sanitized or mythologized to fit a certain narrative, while others were ignored or destroyed in the name of progress. This selective nostalgia for certain parts of American history while ignoring or erasing others is still evident today.

The early 1900s serve as a prime example of this paradox, as Americans both embraced and rejected traditional history and culture in favor of nostalgia for a simpler, more romanticized past. While the desire to preserve and honor America's heritage is certainly admirable, it is important to recognize the selective nature of nostalgia and the danger of erasing or simplifying the complex, nuanced history of our nation.

1910's

The 1910s marked a significant shift in American society, with the nation transitioning from a period of relative peace and prosperity to a decade dominated by World War I and its aftermath. Despite the rapid changes taking place during this time, Americans still felt a strong connection to the past and sought to preserve their memories through nostalgia. This paradox of hating history while loving nostalgia is particularly evident in the 1910s.

One of the most significant examples of nostalgia in the 1910s was the widespread popularity of vaudeville shows. Vaudeville was a form of live entertainment featuring a variety of performers, including singers, dancers, comedians, and magicians. Vaudeville shows were incredibly popular in the early 20th century, drawing large crowds to theaters across the country.

At the heart of vaudeville's appeal was its nostalgic appeal to an earlier time when entertainment was simpler and more wholesome. Many vaudeville acts drew on traditional folk music, comedy routines, and other forms of popular entertainment from earlier eras. This nostalgia for a simpler time was particularly strong during the 1910s, as the country was still reeling from the upheaval caused by World War I.

Another example of the paradox of hating history but loving nostalgia in the 1910s was the growing popularity of historic preservation. The 1910s saw a wave of interest in preserving historic buildings and landmarks, particularly in urban areas. This was driven in part by concerns over the rapid pace of urbanization and the loss of traditional neighborhoods and landmarks.

However, despite this interest in preserving the past, there was little interest in studying or understanding history as an academic subject. History was seen as dry and boring, with little relevance to contemporary life. Instead, Americans focused on preserving the physical artifacts of the past as a way of maintaining a connection to their heritage.

The nostalgia in the 1910s was also evident in popular culture. One of the most iconic examples of this is the popular song "Take Me Out to the Ballgame," which was written in 1908 but became a hit during the 1910s. The song, which celebrates the simple pleasures of going to a baseball game, became a cultural touchstone for Americans of all ages. It spoke to a deep-seated nostalgia for a time when life was simpler and more enjoyable.

Another example of the paradox of hating history but loving nostalgia in the 1910s was the widespread interest in genealogy. Americans were increasingly fascinated with tracing their family history and understanding their ancestry. This interest in genealogy was fueled in part by the growing availability of census records and other historical documents, but it also reflected a desire to connect with the past and understand one's place in the world.

Despite this interest in genealogy, there was little interest in studying or understanding history as an academic subject. History was seen as irrelevant to contemporary life, with little to offer in terms of practical knowledge or skills. Americans were more interested in using history to create a sense of personal identity and connection to the past.

The paradox of hating history but loving nostalgia was evident in the 1910s, as Americans sought to connect with their past in a variety of ways while also rejecting history as an academic subject. The nostalgia for a simpler time was particularly strong during this period, as the country grappled with the upheaval caused by World War I and other major social changes. Whether through popular entertainment, historic preservation, or genealogy, Americans of the 1910s sought to preserve their memories of the past as a way of making sense of the present.

1920's

The 1920s, also known as the Roaring Twenties, was a time of great social and cultural change in the United States. The country had just emerged from World War I and was experiencing a period of economic prosperity. The era was marked by a rebellion against traditional values and an embrace of new freedoms and social norms. While the 1920s may seem like a time when Americans were focused on the present, nostalgia was still prevalent.

One way in which Americans expressed their nostalgia during the 1920s was through the popularity of the Charleston dance craze. The Charleston was a dance that originated in African American communities in the early 1900s, but it gained widespread popularity in the 1920s. The dance was characterized by its high-energy movements and syncopated rhythm, and it quickly became associated with the carefree spirit of the Roaring Twenties. However, the dance also had nostalgic roots, as it was seen as a throwback to the dances of the 1910s, such as the Turkey Trot and the Grizzly Bear.

Another example of nostalgia during the 1920s was the popularity of vintage clothing. Women's fashion in the 1920s was marked by short hemlines, loose silhouettes, and a rejection of the restrictive corsets of the past. However, many women also incorporated elements of vintage fashion into their wardrobes, such as lace collars, brooches, and long gloves. This was seen as a nod to the elegance and sophistication of the Edwardian era, which had ended just a few years prior.

The 1920s also saw a renewed interest in the music of the past, particularly jazz and blues. Jazz had its roots in African American communities in the early 1900s, and it gained popularity among white audiences in the 1920s. However, many jazz musicians also paid homage to the past by incorporating elements of traditional blues and ragtime into their music. For example, Louis Armstrong's Hot Five and Hot Seven recordings from the late 1920s featured songs that drew heavily on blues and ragtime traditions.

Despite the popularity of nostalgia during the 1920s, there was also a sense Americans were eager to leave the past behind and embrace the future. This was reflected in the growing popularity of modern conveniences such as radios, automobiles, and electric appliances. The mass production techniques developed during the 1920s made it possible for more Americans to own these items, and they became symbols of progress and modernity.

So why did Americans during the 1920s both hate history and love nostalgia? One explanation is the rapid social and cultural changes of the era created a sense of disconnection from the past. Many Americans felt the old ways of life were no longer relevant, and they were eager to embrace the new freedoms and opportunities of the present. However, this sense of disconnection also created a longing for the past and a desire to reconnect with the traditions and values of earlier generations.

Another factor may have been the influence of the media. The rise of mass media during the 1920s, particularly radio and film, made it possible for Americans to experience the past in new ways. For example, historical dramas and period films were popular during the era, and they provided a way for Americans to connect with the past without having to live it. Similarly, radio broadcasts of vintage music and shows like "Amos 'n' Andy" provided a way for Americans to experience the culture of earlier generations.

Despite the cultural upheavals of the 1920s, the decade was also characterized by a keen sense of nostalgia. This nostalgia was driven in part by the social and economic changes of the era, which led many Americans to feel disconnected from the traditions and values of their ancestors. The popularity of nostalgic music, literature, and entertainment during this period can be seen as a reaction to this feeling of displacement.

One of the most iconic examples of this nostalgia is the music of the 1920s. While the Jazz Age is often remembered as a time of radical musical experimentation, many popular songs of the era drew on older styles and traditions. For example, the "Tin Pan Alley" songwriters who dominated the popular music scene during this period often drew on 19th-century ballad forms and vaudeville-style humor in their work. Similarly, many jazz musicians of the era, such as Bix Beiderbecke and Benny Goodman, were heavily influenced by the music of earlier eras, including ragtime and the blues.

Another key example of 1920s nostalgia is the popularity of literary and artistic movements ought to revive the aesthetics of earlier eras. The Art Deco movement, for example, drew heavily on the visual language of the Art Nouveau and Arts and Crafts movements of the late 19th and early 20th centuries, while also incorporating motifs from ancient Egypt and other exotic cultures. Similarly, the Harlem Renaissance was characterized by a renewed interest in African American folk traditions, including spirituals and the blues.

At the same time, however, the 1920s also saw the emergence of a more critical attitude toward history and tradition. This attitude was expressed most famously by the Modernist writers and artists of the era, who rejected the conservative values and conventional forms of the past in favor of experimentation and innovation. The work of writers like Ernest Hemingway and F. Scott Fitzgerald, for example, was marked by a sense of disillusionment with the materialistic excesses of the Jazz Age, as well as a critique of the gender and racial inequalities persisted in American society.

In many ways, this ambivalent attitude toward the past and tradition has continued to shape American culture in the years since the 1920s. On the one hand, Americans continue to express a powerful sense of nostalgia for earlier eras, as seen in the popularity of "retro" styles and the continued appeal of historical dramas in film and television. At the same time, however, Americans have also shown a willingness to critically examine the legacies of the past, as seen in the rise of social justice movements and the ongoing debates over Confederate monuments and other symbols of the country's troubled history of racial oppression.

The paradox of American nostalgia and ambivalence toward history and tradition has deep roots in the cultural and social developments of the 1920s. While the era is often remembered as a time of radical change and experimentation, it was also characterized by a sense of displacement and disillusionment led many Americans to seek solace in the familiar rhythms and aesthetics of the past. This nostalgia was not an uncritical embrace of tradition, however, but rather a complex response to the challenges and opportunities of a rapidly changing world.

1930's

The 1930s in America was marked by the Great Depression, which had a profound impact on the country and its people. It was a time of economic hardship, political turmoil, and social unrest, but it was also a time of great creativity and cultural change. During this upheaval, Americans began to embrace nostalgia as a way of coping with the present and finding comfort in the past.

One example of this is the popularity of the "nostalgia craze" in the 1930s. Americans began to look back on the past with a sense of longing and nostalgia, embracing popular music, fashion, and other cultural artifacts from earlier decades. The popularity of swing music, for example, was in part a result of this nostalgia craze, as Americans looked back to the jazz age of the 1920s and sought to recreate the excitement and energy of the time.

Another example of the embrace of nostalgia in the 1930s is the popularity of historical films and literature. Movies like "Gone with the Wind" and "The Adventures of Robin Hood" were hugely popular, transporting audiences to a romanticized version of the past offered an escape from the harsh realities of the present. Similarly, books like "Grapes of Wrath" and "Of Mice and Men" captured the struggles of ordinary people during the Great Depression, but also offered a glimpse into a different time and place.

However, this nostalgia was not just about escapism. It was also a way for Americans to connect with their heritage and find meaning in their history. The New Deal, for example, was a political program aimed to provide relief to those suffering during the Depression. It was also a deliberate effort to create a sense of national identity and pride by connecting Americans to their shared history and culture. The Works Progress Administration, a key component of the New Deal, employed thousands of artists, writers, and musicians to create works of art that celebrated American history and culture. These works, including murals, posters, and music, were displayed in public places like schools and post offices, reinforcing a sense of national identity and pride.

Despite this embrace of nostalgia and history, there was also a sense of disillusionment with the past in the 1930s. The stock market crash of 1929 and the ensuing economic crisis had shattered many Americans' faith in the promise of progress and modernity. This disillusionment was reflected in the literature and art of the time, which often depicted a bleak and desolate world, devoid of hope or meaning.

The 1930s were a decade of significant historical events, including the Great Depression, the rise of authoritarian regimes in Europe, and the start of World War II. Despite this, many Americans look back at the 1930s with nostalgia, seeing it as a simpler time when people pulled together to survive the economic hardships of the era.

One of the most iconic images of the 1930s is of the Dust Bowl, a period of severe dust storms and agricultural devastation affected the Great Plains region of the United States. The Dust Bowl was a result of poor land management practices and a prolonged drought, leading to massive crop failures and widespread poverty. Despite the hardship, many Americans look back on this period with a sense of nostalgia, seeing it as a time when people worked together to survive and help their neighbors.

Another example of the paradox of hating history but loving nostalgia in the 1930s is the popularity of gangster movies. Films such as "Little Caesar," "Public Enemy," and "Scarface" portrayed gangsters as glamorous figures, living outside the law and embodying a certain kind of American individualism. These movies were hugely popular, but they also presented a distorted view of history, glorifying violent criminals and downplaying the actual harm caused by organized crime.

The 1930s also saw the emergence of new forms of popular culture, including comic books and radio dramas. Superman, one of the most iconic comic book characters of all time, was created in 1938, and his adventures were immensely popular among children and adults alike. Radio dramas like "The Shadow" and "The Lone Ranger" captivated audiences with their exciting stories of adventure and heroism. These forms of entertainment helped to create a sense of shared culture and shared experience, something many Americans look back on with fondness.

The paradox of hating history but loving nostalgia is evident in many aspects of American society. From the iconic images of the Dust Bowl to the glamorous portrayal of gangsters in movies, Americans often look back at the past with rose-tinted glasses, seeing it as a simpler time when people pulled together and shared a common culture. While this nostalgia can be comforting, it is important to recognize it is often based on a distorted view of history, and the past was not always as idyllic as we might imagine it to be. By studying history with a critical eye, we can gain a deeper understanding of the past and the present and develop a more nuanced and accurate sense of our shared cultural heritage.

Overall, the 1930s were a time of profound change and upheaval in American society, marked by economic hardship, political turmoil, and social unrest. Americans coped with these challenges by embracing nostalgia as a way of finding comfort in the past and connecting with their heritage. This nostalgia was not just about escapism, but also about finding meaning and purpose in a challenging time and connecting it with a shared sense of national identity and pride.

1940's

The 1940s was a decade marked by the Second World War, and many of the cultural artifacts from this time reflect this tumultuous period in American history. Even though many Americans today may feel distanced from this era, it remains one of the most popular sources of nostalgia in American culture.

One reason for this may be the sense of purpose and national unity Americans felt during this time. The war effort brought together people from all levels of society, and Americans worked together to support the troops and ensure victory against the Axis powers. This sense of unity and shared purpose is often idealized and romanticized in popular culture today.

The music of the 1940s is one of the most iconic examples of this nostalgia. Swing music, which was popularized during this time, has remained a beloved genre of music, even though it is no longer part of the mainstream. Big bands such as Glenn Miller and Benny Goodman dominated the music scene, and songs like "In the Mood" and "Boogie Woogie Bugle Boy" remain classics.

Similarly, the films of the 1940s often reflect the patriotic sentiment of the time. Many films, such as Casablanca and Mrs. Miniver, dealt directly with the war effort, and celebrated the heroism of ordinary Americans who were fighting for their country. These films often feature iconic images of the era, such as the "Rosie the Riveter" character, which has become a symbol of female empowerment and industrial progress.

However, the nostalgia for the 1940s is not just limited to its cultural artifacts. The decade also represents a simpler time in

American history, before the social and political upheavals of the 1960s and 1970s. Many people look back on the 1940s as a time when life was less complicated, and there was a clear sense of right and wrong.

This sense of simplicity is often reflected in the fashion of the era. Women's clothing is often associated with a sense of nostalgia for the 1940s. The "victory roll" hairstyle, the A-line skirt, and the classic pumps are all iconic examples of 1940s fashion and have remained popular to this day.

Additionally, the 1940s saw the rise of suburbanization and the American dream of homeownership. After the war, many soldiers returned home and started families, leading to a boom in suburban development. This era is often associated with the classic image of the white picket fence, and the idea of the perfect American family.

Overall, the nostalgia for the 1940s can be seen as a longing for a simpler time, when there was a clear sense of national purpose and unity. However, it is important to remember the 1940s were not without their own challenges and controversies. The war effort required great sacrifices from Americans, and the country was still grappling with issues of race and gender inequality.

Nevertheless, the cultural artifacts of the 1940s continue to hold a special place in American culture, and the nostalgia for this era remains strong. From swing music to vintage fashion, the 1940s continue to be a source of inspiration and fascination for many Americans.

Throughout the 1940s, America was fighting in World War II, and the country was fully immersed in wartime efforts. The war brought about many significant changes in society, and the decade marked a turning point in American history. While the 1940s were an important and transformative decade for the nation, many Americans today have a fond nostalgia for this era.

One reason for this nostalgia is the perception that the war brought the country together in a way that has not been seen since. Americans rallied around a common cause, and the sacrifices made during the war were seen as noble and necessary for the greater good. This sense of shared sacrifice and national unity is often romanticized and idealized, and many Americans long for a return to this level of unity and purpose.

Another factor contributing to the nostalgia for the 1940s is the popular culture of the time. The decade saw the rise of classic Hollywood films, with stars such as Humphrey Bogart, Lauren Bacall, and Cary Grant becoming iconic figures. These films often depicted an idealized version of American life, with strong, virtuous heroes and happy endings.

Additionally, music from the 1940s, such as swing and big band, remains popular today, and many people associate the era with a simpler, more innocent time.

Despite this nostalgia, the 1940s was also a decade marked by significant social and political upheaval. The war brought about many changes in American society, including the increased participation of women in the workforce and the civil rights movement. The 1940s also saw the internment of Japanese Americans, a shameful chapter in American history is often overlooked or downplayed.

It is worth noting while Americans may express nostalgia for the 1940s, few are interested in studying the complex social and political issues of the time. The popular image of the era as a simpler, more virtuous time is often at odds with the reality of the era's many challenges and struggles. This dichotomy highlights the paradox of American society's relationship with history: while Americans may express a fondness for the past, they are often more interested in the nostalgia and idealized images of the past rather than the complex realities of the time.

During the war, many iconic images emerged have become ingrained in American memory, such as Rosie the Riveter and Uncle Sam. The war also saw the rise of military heroes such as General Dwight D. Eisenhower and General Douglas MacArthur, who became celebrated figures in American history.

However, despite the importance and impact of World War II, the 1940s also saw a rise in nostalgia for the pre-war era.

This nostalgia was reflected in popular culture, as seen in films such as "Meet Me in St. Louis" and "Yankee Doodle Dandy", which romanticized an earlier time. Additionally, the popularity of swing music and ballroom dancing also reflected a desire to escape the realities of war and return to a simpler time.

One reason for the nostalgia of the 1940s may have been the rapid changes that were occurring during this period. The war brought about significant societal changes, including increased opportunities for women in the workforce and advancements in technology. Nostalgia may have been a way for people to cope with the uncertainty and upheaval of the present.

Overall, while the 1940s were a decade of important historical events, including World War II and the post-war economic boom, they were also a time of nostalgia for a simpler past. This paradoxical relationship between American history and nostalgia has continued throughout the decades, reflecting a deep-seated cultural longing for a simpler time while simultaneously acknowledging the importance and impact of the past on the present.

1950's

The 1950s were a time of immense change in America. The country had just emerged from World War II and was now amid a period of prosperity and growth. The economy was booming, and the middle class was expanding. At the same time, there was a great deal of fear and uncertainty in the country, due in large part to the threat of nuclear war with the Soviet Union. Against this backdrop, Americans of the 1950s found comfort in nostalgia.

One of the most iconic symbols of 1950s nostalgia is the television show "Happy Days." Set in the 1950s, the show celebrated an idealized version of American life. The characters were always clean-cut and wholesome, and the show presented a sanitized version of the era glossed over its darker moments. "Happy Days" tapped into a deep-seated nostalgia for a simpler time, when life was perceived as being easier and more carefree.

Another cultural artifact of the 1950s tapped into nostalgia was the rise of the automobile culture. Cars had become an integral part of American life, and they represented freedom, mobility, and adventure. For many Americans, the car represented the promise of the open road, and the ability to explore new places and experience new things. The 1950s also saw the rise of drive-in theaters, which allowed people to watch movies from the comfort of their cars. This created a sense of community and shared experience and was seen to escape the stresses of modern life.

The 1950s also saw a renewed interest in the music of the 1920s and 1930s. Jazz and swing music, which had been popular in the decades before World War II, experienced a resurgence in popularity during the 1950s. Musicians like Louis Armstrong, Duke Ellington, and Benny Goodman became household names once again, and their music provided a soundtrack to the era. This interest in jazz and swing was fueled in part by a desire to recapture the carefree spirit of the pre-war era, and to escape the anxiety and uncertainty of the Cold War.

In addition to these cultural artifacts, the 1950s also saw a renewed interest in historic preservation. As cities and towns across America experienced rapid growth and development, many people became concerned about the loss of historic buildings and landmarks. This led to a renewed interest in preserving America's architectural heritage, and to the creation of organizations like the National Trust for Historic Preservation. This interest in historic preservation was driven in part by a desire to hold on to the past, and to maintain a connection to an earlier, simpler time.

The 1950s were a time of profound change in America, marked by both prosperity and anxiety. Against this backdrop, Americans found comfort in nostalgia. The television show "Happy Days," the rise of automobile culture, the resurgence of jazz and swing music, and the renewed interest in historic preservation all tapped into a deep-seated desire to hold on to the past, and to recapture a simpler, more carefree time. This paradox, of hating history but loving nostalgia, reflected the anxiety and uncertainty of the era, and of a desire to escape the stresses of modern life.

In addition to the romanticized view of the 1950s in popular culture, there are other factors contribute to Americans' nostalgia for this decade. For example, the 1950s saw the rise of the suburbs and the baby boom, which represented a prosperous and optimistic time for many Americans. The decade also witnessed the beginning of the civil rights movement, which while tumultuous, led to considerable progress in achieving greater racial equality.

Despite these positive developments, the 1950s also saw the perpetuation of many oppressive social norms, such as gender roles and racial segregation. In hindsight, it is easy to view this decade through rose-colored glasses, but it is important to remember the complex and nuanced realities of the time. Understanding history in its full context can help us appreciate progress and identify areas where further change is needed.

The paradox of Americans' simultaneous disdain for history and love of nostalgia can be attributed to a variety of factors, including a lack of engaging and relevant history education, a desire for simplified and idealized versions of the past, and the human tendency to romanticize the "good old days." However, it is important for individuals and society to acknowledge and confront the complexities of history to gain a deeper understanding of our present and shape a more equitable future.

Another reason for the popularity of nostalgia in the 1950s was the rise of television. Television became a popular household item and shows like "I Love Lucy" and "Leave It to Beaver" depicted a romanticized version of the 1950s, where everything was perfect and wholesome. These shows presented a nostalgic view of the past that was appealing to viewers, and they contributed to the nostalgia for the 1950s continues to this day.

In addition to television, the emergence of rock and roll music in the 1950s also contributed to the popularity of nostalgia for that decade. Rock and roll music had a significant impact on American culture and played a key role in the social and cultural changes of the time. It was seen as rebellious and nonconformist, which appealed to many young people. However, as time passed, rock and roll became more mainstream, and its rebellious nature faded. As a result, many people began to associate rock and roll with the innocence and simplicity of the 1950s, and it became a symbol of that decade's nostalgia.

Finally, the 1950s marked a period of economic prosperity and stability in the United States. The post-World War II era saw a booming economy and a growing middle class, which led to increased consumerism and a greater focus on material goods. This economic prosperity created a sense of stability and security that was not present in the preceding decades. As a result, many people look back on the 1950s with nostalgia for a time when the economy was booming, and the future looked bright.

The paradox of Americans hating history, but loving nostalgia can be attributed to a variety of factors. One reason is the human tendency to view the past through rose-colored glasses, remembering the good times and forgetting the bad. Additionally, the influence of popular culture, including movies, television, and music, plays a significant role in shaping our perceptions of the past. Finally, economic and social factors also contribute to the nostalgia for past decades, particularly those that were marked by stability and prosperity. By understanding the reasons behind this paradox, we can gain a greater appreciation for the role nostalgia plays in American society and culture.

1960's

The 1960s were a decade of social upheaval and transformation in American history. From the Civil Rights Movement to the Vietnam War protests, Americans witnessed significant changes in their society would shape the future of the nation. However, despite the importance of these events, many Americans today tend to view the 1960s through rose-colored glasses, romanticizing the era as a time of peace, love, and freedom. This paradox of hating history but loving nostalgia is particularly evident in our cultural representations of the decade.

One of the most iconic symbols of the 1960s is the hippie counterculture. The hippie movement emerged as a response to the conformity and consumerism of post-war America, and it quickly became associated with anti-war protests, drug use, and free love. Today, the image of the hippie is often celebrated as a symbol of rebellion and freedom, but this romanticized view ignores the more complex realities of the time. For example, many members of the counterculture were also involved in political activism and social justice movements, such as the Civil Rights Movement and the feminist movement. The hippie movement was not just about hedonism and escapism; it was also a response to the injustices of the time.

Another aspect of the 1960s often romanticized is the music of the era. The Beatles, Bob Dylan, and Jimi Hendrix are just a few of the musicians whose songs have come to define the decade. However, it is important to remember the music of the 1960s was not just about catchy tunes and groovy dance moves. Many of the songs of the era were political and socially conscious, addressing issues such as war, racism, and poverty. For example, Bob Dylan's "Blowin' in the Wind" became an anthem for the Civil Rights Movement, while Jimi Hendrix's "Machine Gun" was a commentary on the brutality of war. By focusing only on the feel-good hits of the era, we miss the deeper meanings and messages these songs were trying to convey.

One of the most noteworthy events of the 1960s was the Civil Rights Movement, which sought to end racial discrimination and segregation in the United States. This movement was marked by powerful protests and acts of civil disobedience, such as the Montgomery Bus Boycott and the March on Washington. However, the way we remember the Civil Rights Movement today often obscures the harsh realities of the time. For example, many Americans today view Martin Luther King Jr. as a hero and a champion of equality, but during his lifetime he faced intense opposition and hostility. The same can be said for other Civil Rights activists, such as Malcolm X and the Black Panthers, who were often demonized by the media and the government.

The Vietnam War was another defining event of the 1960s, and it remains one of the most controversial conflicts in American history. The anti-war movement was a prominent feature of the era, with protests and demonstrations taking place across the country. The famous Kent State shootings in 1970, in which National Guardsmen opened fire on unarmed students, is just one example of the violence that marked the era. Despite the divisiveness of the time, many Americans today view the Vietnam War protests as a noble and courageous stand against an unjust war.

The paradox of hating history but loving nostalgia is particularly evident in our cultural representations of the 1960s. Although the decade was marked by significant social and political changes, many Americans today view the era through a rose-colored lens, romanticizing the hippie counterculture, the music of the era, and the Civil Rights and anti-war movements. While it is understandable to want to celebrate the positive aspects of the past,

The 1960s were a decade of momentous change and upheaval in American society. This was a time of civil rights activism, anti-war protests, and a counterculture that rejected the values of the older generation. Many Americans look back on this time with nostalgia, but why is it they often fail to appreciate the historical significance of these events?

One reason for this may be the events of the 1960s are often romanticized and simplified in popular culture. The image of the "hippie" or the "protester" has become a cliché, and many people today view the era through a lens of nostalgia emphasizes the music, fashion, and pop culture of the time. However, this nostalgic view can obscure the complexity and nuance of the social and political issues of the time.

For example, the civil rights movement of the 1960s is often remembered as a heroic struggle for justice and equality. While this is certainly true, it is important to remember the movement was also highly controversial and polarizing at the time. Many white Americans saw the civil rights movement as a threat to their way of life, and some even supported violent resistance to desegregation and equal rights.

Similarly, the anti-war protests of the 1960s are often celebrated as a courageous stand against an unjust war. However, at the time, many Americans saw the protests as unpatriotic and even treasonous. This perspective is often forgotten in the nostalgic view of the 1960s, which emphasizes the heroism of the protesters rather than the divisions and conflicts that existed in society.

Another reason for the paradoxical relationship between Americans and history is the way in which history is taught in schools. Many students are required to memorize a series of dates, events, and names without fully understanding the broader context or significance of these facts. This approach can make history seem dry and irrelevant, leading many students to develop a dislike or even a hatred of the subject.

Furthermore, the way in which history is taught often reinforces a traditional, Eurocentric view of American history that marginalizes the experiences and contributions of marginalized groups such as women, people of color, and LGBTQ+ individuals. This can create a sense of alienation and disconnection from history for those who do not see themselves reflected in the stories that are told.

In contrast, nostalgia allows individuals to selectively choose and romanticize certain aspects of the past they find appealing, while ignoring the less pleasant realities. Nostalgia is a form of escapism from the present, and it provides comfort and security in uncertain times. This can be especially appealing during times of social and political upheaval, when many people feel anxious or disconnected from their communities.

In the case of the 1960s, nostalgia for this era can be seen as a reaction to the political and social upheavals of recent years. The current political climate has been marked by divisions and polarization, and many people feel disillusioned with the current state of American society. In this context, the idealism and activism of the 1960s can provide a comforting and inspiring alternative to the present.

The paradox of why Americans hate history, but love nostalgia can be attributed to a variety of factors, including the oversimplification and romanticization of historical events in popular culture, the way in which history is taught in schools, and the appeal of nostalgia as a form of escapism. By understanding these factors, we can begin to appreciate the importance of studying history and the complexities of the past, while also recognizing the value of nostalgia as a source of comfort and inspiration in uncertain times.

Another reason the 1960s are often viewed nostalgically is because of the cultural and societal changes that occurred during this time. The Civil Rights Movement and the Women's Rights Movement were gaining momentum, challenging the traditional power structures of American society. The counterculture movement was also in full swing, with young people rejecting mainstream values and norms.

One of the most iconic moments of the 1960s was the Woodstock Music Festival in August 1969. It was a three-day music festival held in upstate New York and attracted over 400,000 people (about half the population of Delaware). The festival has become a symbol of the 1960s counterculture and is often referenced in popular culture.

However, despite the fond memories many Americans have of the 1960s, there were also significant challenges and tragedies during this time. The Vietnam War was raging, causing widespread protests and social unrest. In 1963, President John F. Kennedy was assassinated, leaving the nation in shock and mourning.

The paradox of Americans' love of nostalgia but disdain for history can be attributed to the selective memory nostalgia allows. It is easier to remember the positive aspects of a time and forget the negative, especially if those negative aspects do not directly impact one's firsthand experiences. Additionally, nostalgia is often associated with feelings of comfort and familiarity, whereas history can be complex and uncomfortable to confront.

Overall, the paradox of why Americans hate history, but love nostalgia is a complex issue with no easy answers. However, by examining the specific reasons why certain decades are viewed nostalgically, we can begin to understand the factors that contribute to this paradox.

1970's

The 1970s were a decade of significant change in American society. From the end of the Vietnam War to the Watergate scandal and the rise of disco music, the 1970s were marked by many pivotal moments that continue to shape our country today. Despite this, many Americans tend to view the decade through a lens of nostalgia, often forgetting or glossing over the challenges and controversies of the time.

One major factor that contributes to Americans' love of nostalgia for the 1970s is the cultural impact of the decade. From iconic films like The Godfather and Star Wars to classic television shows like All in the Family and Happy Days, the 1970s produced a wealth of beloved cultural touchstones that still resonate with audiences today. Many of these pop culture artifacts have become ingrained in the American psyche, embodying a sense of nostalgia for a simpler time.

However, this nostalgia often overlooks the complex social and political issues of the decade. For example, the Vietnam War continued to drag on for much of the early 1970s, despite widespread protests and growing opposition to the conflict. The Watergate scandal also dominated headlines in the latter part of the decade, exposing corruption at the highest levels of government and eroding public trust in political institutions.

In addition to these events, the 1970s were also marked by significant social change, including the ongoing struggle for civil rights and the rise of feminism. The Women's Liberation movement gained momentum throughout the decade, leading to landmark legislation like Title IX, which prohibited gender discrimination in education. The gay rights movement also began to gain traction in the 1970s, culminating in the 1979 March on Washington for Lesbian and Gay Rights.

Despite these important developments, many Americans tend to remember the 1970s as a time of peace, love, and disco. This selective memory can be attributed to several factors, including the way in which history is taught in American schools. Often, history classes focus on memorization of dates and names rather than on understanding the broader social, political, and economic context of a given period. As a result, many Americans develop a shallow understanding of history that lacks nuance and depth.

Another factor that contributes to Americans' love of nostalgia for the 1970s is the fact the decade marked the beginning of the decline of the American middle class. In the 1970s, the U.S. experienced an economic downturn, and wages stagnated for many workers. This economic insecurity, combined with a sense of disillusionment with political institutions, led many Americans to long for a simpler, more stable time. For some, this longing takes the form of a nostalgia for the 1950s, a decade that is often viewed as a golden age of American prosperity and social stability.

Americans' love of nostalgia for the 1970s is a paradoxical phenomenon that speaks to the complex relationship between memory and history. While many Americans view the decade through rose-colored glasses, selectively remembering the cultural touchstones of the time while glossing over its social and political challenges, the legacy of the 1970s continues to shape our country in profound ways. By acknowledging both the nostalgia and the complexities of the past, we can gain a more nuanced understanding of American history and its ongoing impact on our society today.

Throughout the 1970s, nostalgia for the 1950s continued to be popular in American society, as evidenced by the success of TV shows like "Happy Days" and movies like "American

Graffiti." These shows and films depicted a simpler time in American history, one that was seen as more innocent and wholesome than the tumultuous 1960s. However, there was also a growing sense of disillusionment with American society during this time, as the Vietnam War continued to drag on and the Watergate scandal eroded people's trust in the government.

One example of this nostalgia is the popularity of the TV show "Happy Days," which premiered in 1974 and ran for 11 seasons. The show was set in the 1950s and depicted the lives of the Cunningham family and their friends, who spent their time hanging out at Arnold's Drive-In and listening to rock 'n' roll music. The show's popularity was a testament to the enduring appeal of the 1950s in American culture, as well as a reflection of the desire for a simpler time in the face of the social and political upheaval of the 1960s.

Another example is the success of the movie "American Graffiti," which was released in 1973 and became a huge box office hit. The film, which was directed by George Lucas, was set in 1962 and followed a group of teenagers as they cruised around town and listened to music on their car radios. Like "Happy Days," "American Graffiti" was a celebration of a simpler time in American history, one that was seen as more innocent and carefree than the present day.

However, even as Americans looked back with nostalgia to the 1950s and early 1960s, there was also a growing sense of disillusionment with American society during the 1970s. The Vietnam War continued to drag on, with no end in sight, and the Watergate scandal eroded people's trust in the government. There were also economic challenges, as the country struggled with inflation and rising unemployment rates.

This disillusionment was reflected in the music of the era, as artists like Bruce Springsteen and Bob Dylan wrote songs about the struggles of working-class Americans and the disillusionment with the American Dream. Springsteen's 1975 album "Born to Run" was a critical and commercial success, and the title track became an anthem for young Americans who were looking for a way out of their small towns and into a better life.

The 1970s were a decade of contradictions in American society. On the one hand, there was a strong sense of nostalgia for the 1950s and early 1960s, as Americans looked back with longing to a simpler time in the nation's history.

On the other hand, there was a growing sense of disillusionment with American society, as the Vietnam War dragged on and the Watergate scandal eroded people's trust in the government. This paradox continues to this day, as Americans struggle to reconcile their love of nostalgia with their complicated relationship with the past.

1980's

The 1980s were a decade of contradictions for Americans. It was a time of economic growth, technological advancements, and cultural change, but it was also a time of political turmoil, social unrest, and international tensions. Despite these complexities, the 1980s remain a popular topic for nostalgia among many Americans.

The 1980s saw a continuation of the cultural nostalgia that had begun in the 1970s, as people looked back on the simpler times of the 1950s and 1960s. This nostalgia was reflected in popular films such as "Back to the Future," which took viewers on a journey back in time to the 1950s, and television shows like "Happy Days" and "The Wonder Years," which celebrated the innocence and optimism of the past.

At the same time, the 1980s was a decade of rapid technological change, and many of the cultural touchstones of the time were tied to these innovative technologies. The personal computer became a household item, video games entered the mainstream, and music videos transformed the way people experienced music. This technological revolution is still remembered fondly by many people, and the music, movies, and television shows of the time continue to be popular.

However, despite the prevalence of nostalgia for the 1980s, many people also have a complicated relationship with this decade. It was a time of significant social and political change, as the civil rights and feminist movements continued to gain ground, and the AIDS crisis emerged as a major public health concern. Many people who lived through the 1980s remember it as a time of political conservatism, economic inequality, and environmental degradation.

One example of this complicated relationship with the 1980s is the continued popularity of the John Hughes movies, such as "The Breakfast Club" and "Ferris Bueller's Day Off." These movies are beloved for their depictions of teenage angst and rebellion, but they also reinforce stereotypes about gender and social class. Similarly, the music of the 1980s is remembered for its catchy melodies and danceable beats, but it also perpetuated many of the social and cultural norms of the time, including rampant consumerism and the objectification of women.

The paradox of the 1980s, then, is that while many Americans continue to love the cultural artifacts of the decade, they are also aware of its limitations and contradictions. This paradox is reflected in the ongoing debates over the legacies of figures such as Ronald Reagan, who is remembered by some as a hero of conservative values and by others as a symbol of the worst excesses of the decade.

The paradox of why Americans hate history, but love nostalgia is particularly evident in the 1980s. While this decade is often celebrated for its cultural innovations and technological advancements, it was also a time of significant social and political upheaval. The continued popularity of the cultural artifacts of the 1980s reflects both a desire to recapture the optimism and innocence of the past and a recognition of the complexities and contradictions of the decade.

Another aspect of 1980s nostalgia is the rise of nostalgia for the 1950s. This was a decade marked by the popularity of rock 'n' roll music, drive-in movies, and the beginning of the civil rights movement. The 1980s saw a resurgence of interest in the styles, music, and culture of the 1950s, which was reflected in films like "Back to the Future" and TV shows like "Happy Days."

The 1980s also saw the rise of nostalgia for the Cold War era. While the threat of nuclear war loomed large during this time, it also represented a simpler time for many Americans, who longed for a return to the days when the United States was seen as a world leader and the enemy was clearly defined. This nostalgia was reflected in films like "Red Dawn" and "Top Gun," which celebrated the heroism of American soldiers and the military.

The paradox of why Americans hate history, but love nostalgia is a complex and multifaceted phenomenon can be traced back to the early days of American history. While Americans may not be interested in the details of the past, they are drawn to the nostalgia of a simpler time when life was less complicated and more innocent. From the 1880s to the 1980s, this nostalgia has taken many forms, from Wild

West shows to 1950s rock 'n' roll to Cold War heroism. By understanding the role of nostalgia in American culture, we can gain a better understanding of why Americans are drawn to certain cultural touchstones and what it says about our values and aspirations as a society.

One of the most significant historical events of the 1980s was the end of the Cold War. The US and the Soviet Union had been in a tense standoff for decades, with each country holding a vast nuclear arsenal aimed at the other. However, under President Ronald Reagan's leadership, the US began a campaign of military buildup and strategic economic pressure on the Soviet Union, which led to the collapse of the Soviet government in 1991.

Despite this significant turning point in world history, many Americans of the 1980s focused more on the cultural changes happening in their own country. This was the decade of big hair, shoulder pads, and the birth of the MTV generation. Pop culture was dominated by the rise of music icons such as Michael Jackson and Madonna, and movies such as "E.T." and "Back to the Future" became instant classics.

Many people today look back on the 1980s with nostalgia, remembering the music, fashion, and movies with fondness. However, at the time, there was little focus on the historical significance of the events happening around them. Instead, the focus was on personal enjoyment and individual expression.

This paradox of loving nostalgia but hating history can be seen as a reflection of the broader cultural shifts that were happening in the US during this time. The rise of consumer culture and individualism meant people were more focused on their own experiences and desires than on the larger historical context in which they were living.

Furthermore, the 1980s were a time of rapid technological change, with the rise of personal computers, cell phones, and other gadgets that promised to make life easier and more efficient. This technological optimism further reinforced the idea the future was more important than the past and history was something to be left behind rather than learned from.

The 1980s were a time of significant historical change, but this change was often overshadowed by the focus on individualism, consumerism, and technological progress. While many people today look back on the decade with nostalgia, it is essential to remember the larger historical context in which these cultural shifts occurred and the lessons that can be learned from studying that context.

1990's

The 1990s were a time of great change in America, marked by technological advances, globalization, and social upheaval. Despite these changes, many Americans remain nostalgic for the past, particularly for the cultural touchstones of their childhood and adolescence. From the music of the '90s to the movies and TV shows that defined the era, Americans often look back with fondness on the pop culture of the decade.

However, this nostalgia is often divorced from the reality of the time, which was marked by political and economic instability, cultural divisions, and other challenges. One of the defining moments of the 1990s was the Gulf War, which marked the first major military conflict since Vietnam.

The war was widely covered in the media, and many Americans supported the military action. However, the aftermath of the war was marked by political turmoil, as President George H.W. Bush's popularity plummeted amid a weak economy and concerns over his handling of domestic issues. The 1992 election saw the rise of Bill Clinton, whose campaign was marked by a focus on the economy and the slogan "It's the economy, stupid." Clinton's presidency was marked by several significant accomplishments, including the passage of the North American Free Trade Agreement (NAFTA) and the establishment of the Family and Medical Leave Act. However, his presidency was also marked by controversy, including the Monica Lewinsky scandal, which led to his impeachment by the House of Representatives in 1998.

Culturally, the 1990s were defined by a few trends, including the rise of grunge music, the popularity of hip-hop, and the emergence of teen culture as a dominant force in entertainment. Shows like Beverly Hills, 90210 and movies like Clueless and Scream were hugely popular, while the rise of the internet and the emergence of online communities like AOL and Prodigy created new opportunities for communication and connection. Despite these cultural touchstones, however, the '90s were also marked by cultural divisions, particularly around issues of race and identity. The Los Angeles riots of 1992, sparked by the acquittal of police officers in the beating of Rodney King, highlighted the deep-seated tensions and inequalities in American society.

Despite these challenges, however, many Americans look back on the 1990s with fondness, particularly for the pop culture of the era. The music of the '90s continues to be popular, with bands like Nirvana and Pearl Jam enjoying enduring popularity. TV shows like Friends and Seinfeld remain beloved by many, while movies like Forrest Gump and Titanic continue to be popular favorites. This nostalgia for the '90s is often tied to a sense of longing for a simpler time when life seemed less complicated and less fraught with uncertainty.

But why do Americans love nostalgia so much? One explanation is it offers a sense of comfort and familiarity in a world that can often feel chaotic and uncertain. Nostalgia allows us to connect with a shared past and to feel a sense of belonging to a larger community. It can also offer a way to escape the stresses and pressures of the present, by transporting us to a time when things seemed simpler and more manageable.

However, nostalgia can also be problematic, particularly when it leads us to romanticize the past or to overlook its flaws and complexities. This is particularly true when it comes to historical events, which are often presented in simplified or distorted ways in popular culture. By focusing on the surface-level aspects of the past, we risk overlooking the nuances and complexities that shaped the world we live in today.

In the 1990s, we see a resurgence of nostalgia for the 1960s and 1970s. This can be seen in various forms of media, such as music, TV shows, and movies. One example of this is the popular TV show "That '70s Show," which aired from 1998 to 2006. The show was set in the 1970s and depicted the lives of a group of teenagers in a small town in Wisconsin. The show's popularity can be attributed to its humorous depiction of the 1970s and its relatable characters.

Another example of 1990s nostalgia is the popularity of grunge music, which was influenced by the punk rock of the 1970s. Grunge bands such as Nirvana, Soundgarden, and Pearl Jam rose to prominence in the early 1990s and brought a new wave of rock music to the forefront of American culture. The lyrics of grunge songs often reflected feelings of angst and dissatisfaction, which resonated with many young Americans at the time.

In addition to music and TV shows, 1990s nostalgia was also evident in fashion. The popularity of retro clothing styles, such as bell-bottoms and tie-dye shirts, reflected a desire to relive the fashion trends of the 1960s and 1970s. This trend was seen not only among young people but also in mainstream fashion, with designers incorporating retro styles into their collections.

Overall, the 1990s saw a continued fascination with nostalgia for past decades. Americans in this decade were still seemingly disinterested in history as a subject but continued to embrace nostalgia to connect with the past and find comfort in a familiar cultural landscape.

Another reason for the popularity of nostalgia in the 1990s was the emergence of the Internet and the rise of digital technology. With the increasing accessibility of the Internet and the ability to connect with people and content from the past, nostalgia became a more common and even celebrated aspect of American culture. For example, the creation of websites dedicated to the preservation and celebration of nostalgic content such as classic television shows, movies, and music, allowed people to relive their childhoods and connect with others who shared similar memories and experiences.

Additionally, in the 1990s, the Baby Boomer generation, who were born between 1946 and 1964, began to reach middle age, leading to an increased interest in nostalgia for their youth. This generation, which had experienced significant social and political upheaval during their formative years, often romanticized their past and looked back on it with fondness. This led to a resurgence of interest in 1960s and 1970s counterculture, music, and fashion, with many Baby Boomers seeking to recapture the spirit of their youth.

The paradox of Americans' love for nostalgia and hatred for history can be attributed to a variety of factors. While history may be viewed as dry and disconnected from our individual experiences, nostalgia allows us to connect with our past and relive memories that have shaped who we are. Moreover, nostalgia often serves as a form of escapism from the present, providing a sense of comfort and familiarity in an uncertain and rapidly changing world. With the emergence of modern technologies and the aging of the Baby Boomer generation, the popularity of nostalgia is likely to continue, even as Americans remain largely disinterested in studying and learning from their history.

2000's

The 2000s saw a surge of nostalgia for the 1980s and 1990s. It was a decade of growth and change in terms of technology and the economy, but also a period of war and political division. With the rise of the internet and social media, nostalgia became even more prevalent in American society. Many people used online platforms to reminisce about the past, and popular culture also reflected a desire for simpler times.

One example of this nostalgia can be seen in the popularity of music from the 1980s and 1990s. Bands like Journey, Bon Jovi, and Guns N' Roses experienced renewed popularity in the early 2000s. This nostalgia extended to television shows and movies from the 1980s and 1990s as well, with remakes and reboots of popular franchises like "Transformers" and "Teenage Mutant Ninja Turtles."

Another way nostalgia was evident in the 2000s was through fashion. Many people began wearing clothes reminiscent of the 1980s and 1990s, with trends like high-waisted jeans, neon colors, and oversized glasses making a comeback. This nostalgia also extended to technology, with the resurgence of vinyl records and the popularity of retro gaming consoles like the Nintendo Entertainment System.

While this nostalgia was prevalent in the 2000s, Americans still struggled with a disinterest in history. In fact, many historians noted the 2000s saw a continued decline in the teaching of history in schools. A 2007 survey found fewer than half of American students could correctly identify the century in which the American Civil War occurred.

So why do Americans love nostalgia but hate history? One explanation is nostalgia allows people to idealize and romanticize the past, while history forces people to confront uncomfortable truths. Nostalgia provides a sense of comfort and familiarity, while history can be challenging and unsettling.

In addition, nostalgia often focuses on pop culture and consumerism, which can be more appealing to many Americans than the sometimes dry and academic study of history. Pop culture provides a sense of shared experiences and a connection to a broader cultural zeitgeist, while history can feel disconnected and irrelevant to people's daily lives.

Another factor that contributes to this paradox is the way history is taught in schools. Many students report finding history classes boring or irrelevant, and the focus on memorization of facts and dates can make it difficult for students to connect with the subject matter. Additionally, history is often taught as a series of isolated events rather than a cohesive narrative, which can make it harder for students to see the relevance and importance of what they are learning.

Despite these challenges, it is important for Americans to understand and appreciate their history. By understanding the past, people can gain insights into the present and make more informed decisions about the future. History also provides a sense of identity and a connection to a larger community, which can be valuable in times of uncertainty and upheaval.

One way to bridge the gap between nostalgia and history is to use nostalgia as a gateway to learn about the past. For example, a person who is interested in 1980s pop culture could explore the social and political context of that decade, gaining a deeper understanding of the forces that shaped the world they grew up in. By making history more relevant and relatable to people's lives, it may be possible to increase interest and engagement in the subject.

Another reason for the love of nostalgia over history may be the way we consume information today. With the rise of the internet and social media, information is shared at a rapid pace, and attention spans are shorter than ever. People are more likely to consume bite-sized pieces of information that are easy to digest rather than dive into the complexities of history.

In addition, the 2000s saw the rise of nostalgia marketing, where companies use nostalgic references to sell products. For example, Coca-Cola's "Share a Coke" campaign, where people could buy bottles with their names on them, or the resurgence of classic brands like Polaroid cameras and record players. These marketing strategies tap into people's fond memories of the past and make them feel nostalgic, even for things they may not have experienced themselves.

Overall, the paradox of why Americans hate history, but love nostalgia is a complex issue with many contributing factors. It could be due to a lack of interest in traditional historical education, a desire to escape the stress of modern life, or a preference for easily digestible information. It could also be due to the powerful emotional connections people have to their personal memories and experiences. Whatever the reason, nostalgia will continue to hold a special place in

American culture, even as history remains a neglected subject in many educational settings.

Another example of nostalgia in the 2000s was the rise of vintage fashion. During this decade, fashion trends from past decades became popular again, with people looking for unique styles and designs from previous eras. Fashion designers started to incorporate retro styles into their collections, and vintage clothing stores became more popular. The 2000s saw the revival of 1980s fashion trends like neon colors, leg warmers, and shoulder pads, as well as 1970s styles such as bell-bottoms and platform shoes.

Nostalgia was also evident in the popularity of retro video games and consoles. In 2006, Nintendo released the Wii, which featured classic games from previous consoles like the Nintendo Entertainment System and Super Nintendo. Other gaming companies like Sega and Atari released collections of classic games from the 1980s and 1990s, allowing people to relive their childhood memories of playing these games.

Americans have a complex relationship with history and nostalgia. While many people may find history boring or irrelevant, they often enjoy looking back at past eras with a sense of nostalgia. This is evident in the popularity of retro fashion, music, movies, and video games. Nostalgia allows people to revisit the past and relive positive memories, even if those memories are not always accurate representations of historical reality. It is important to recognize the distinction between nostalgia and history, and to use both perspectives to gain a more complete understanding of the past and its impact on the present.

2010's

The 2010s were a decade of rapid change and technological advancement in the United States. From the rise of social media to the proliferation of smartphones, Americans witnessed and participated in several transformative events that will undoubtedly shape the course of history for years to come. However, despite this wealth of new experiences and information, Americans still harbor a deep-seated ambivalence towards history, preferring instead to dwell on the past through the lens of nostalgia.

One example of this paradoxical relationship between Americans and history in the 2010s can be seen in the popularity of the TV show "Stranger Things". Set in the 1980s, the show serves as a love letter to that decade, filled with references to iconic movies, TV shows, and pop culture figures from that era. Despite being set in the past, however, "Stranger Things" resonated with audiences in the present, with its themes of friendship, family, and the supernatural striking a chord with viewers of all ages. In a way, the show's popularity can be seen as a manifestation of Americans' desire to connect with the past, even as they grapple with the challenges and uncertainties of the present.

Another example of this paradox can be found in the way Americans commemorated the 10th anniversary of the 9/11 attacks in 2011. While the attacks themselves were a traumatic event Americans would rather forget, the anniversary was marked by a wave of nostalgia for the sense of unity and patriotism that emerged in the aftermath of the tragedy. From memorial services to public gatherings, Americans came together to remember those who lost their lives and to reflect on the impact the attacks had on the country. While this reflection was undoubtedly important, it is worth noting it was focused on the immediate aftermath of the attacks, rather than the broader historical context that led to them.

Yet another example of this paradox can be seen in the way Americans grappled with issues of race and inequality in the 2010s. Despite the country's long and complicated history of racial discrimination and injustice, many Americans seemed resistant to engaging with this history head-on. Instead, discussions of race and inequality often took on a nostalgic tone, with many people longing for a bygone era of racial harmony that never truly existed. This nostalgia was reflected in everything from popular TV shows like "Mad Men" and "The Marvelous Mrs. Maisel", which hearkened back to a time when traditional gender and racial hierarchies were more firmly entrenched, to political rhetoric that romanticized a vision of America that was more homogeneous and "traditional".

Taken together, these examples illustrate the complex and often contradictory relationship Americans have with history and nostalgia in the 21st century. While many Americans are quick to dismiss history as dry and boring, they remain deeply connected to the past through the lens of nostalgia, and often long for a simpler, more idyllic time that may or may not have ever existed. This paradox is rooted in a number of varied factors, including Americans' tendency towards individualism and their cultural preference for the new and the novel over the old and the familiar. Nevertheless, it is a paradox that will continue to shape American society and culture for years to come, as Americans grapple with the challenges and opportunities of the present while simultaneously looking back to the past for guidance and inspiration.

As we move into the 2010s, the trend of loving nostalgia and being indifferent to history continued. Social media platforms like Facebook, Twitter, and Instagram became increasingly popular, allowing people to easily share memories and experiences from their past.

In terms of popular culture, we saw a resurgence of 90s fashion and music, with artists like Drake and Kanye West sampling old songs and wearing vintage clothing. Reboots and sequels of popular 90s TV shows and movies like "Full House" and "Jurassic Park" were also popular among audiences.

Similarly, the rise of the "hipster" subculture saw a revival of vintage clothing, vinyl records, and old-fashioned cocktails. This obsession with the past was often seen as a rejection of the modern, fast-paced world we live in today.

However, when it came to current events and politics, many Americans remained disengaged. In a 2014 survey, only 36% of Americans could name all three branches of government, and just 38% knew which party controlled the House of Representatives.

This lack of interest in current events was also reflected in voter turnout rates, which remained low in the 2010s. In the 2016 presidential election, only 55% of eligible voters cast a ballot, a number that had not been seen since the 1990s.

So, why do Americans hate history but love nostalgia? One explanation is nostalgia allows us to remember the good times and forget about the bad. It is easy to look back at the past with rose-colored glasses and forget about the struggles and injustices that occurred.

History, on the other hand, forces us to confront the uncomfortable truths about our past and present. It requires us to acknowledge the mistakes and injustices of our ancestors, and to work towards a better future.

Even though Americans generally dislike history, nostalgia remains an important part of American culture. This paradox is best exemplified by the 2016 election of Donald Trump, who campaigned on a slogan of "Make America Great Again." Trump's campaign tapped into a sense of nostalgia for a mythical past when America was a more prosperous, powerful, and virtuous nation. Although this nostalgia was not shared by all Americans, it did resonate with a sizable portion of the population, particularly those who felt left behind by globalization and the changing demographics of the country.

But why do Americans love nostalgia so much, even as they reject the study of history? One explanation is nostalgia allows people to escape from the complexities and uncertainties of the present and immerse themselves in a simpler, more idealized past. By indulging in nostalgia, people can focus on the positive aspects of the past while ignoring the negative ones. This is particularly true for those who feel disillusioned by the current situation and are looking for a sense of meaning and purpose in their lives.

Another explanation is nostalgia is often tied to identity and community. In an increasingly diverse and globalized world, many people feel disconnected from their roots and long for a sense of belonging and identity. Nostalgia for a particular time and place can provide a sense of continuity and connection to the past, which in turn can strengthen one's sense of identity and community.

Furthermore, nostalgia is often fueled by popular culture and media, which can serve as a bridge between the past and the present. For example, movies, television shows, and music from past decades can evoke strong feelings of nostalgia for those who experienced them in their youth. In some cases, this nostalgia can be so powerful it creates a sense of community among people who have shared similar cultural experiences.

Despite the enduring appeal of nostalgia, it is important to recognize it is not a substitute for the study of history. Nostalgia can be an important part of personal and collective identity, but it is not a substitute for a critical understanding of the past. The study of history allows us to better understand the complexities of the past and how they shape the present. It also allows us to learn from the mistakes and successes of previous generations and apply these lessons to our own lives.

The paradox of why Americans hate history, but love nostalgia is a complex and multifaceted issue. It is rooted in a variety of factors, including a desire for escape, a search for identity and community, and the influence of popular culture and media. While nostalgia can be a powerful and positive force in our lives, it is also not a substitute for the study of history. By embracing both nostalgia and history, we can gain a deeper understanding of ourselves and our society, and work towards a brighter future.

2020's

As we move into the 2020s, the paradox of why Americans hate history, but love nostalgia continues to persist. With the ever-increasing amount of information and digital archives available, it may seem surprising that many Americans still struggle to connect with and appreciate history. Instead, we see a rise in nostalgia-driven media and entertainment that romanticizes past eras.

One example of this is the resurgence of 90s nostalgia. TV shows like Friends and movies like Clueless have seen a resurgence in popularity, as have iconic toys from the era such as Tamagotchis and Pogs. The 90s are often romanticized as a simpler time before the rise of social media and smartphones. However, this nostalgia overlooks the many social and political issues that plagued the decade, including the O.J. Simpson trial and the Rodney King riots.

Another example is the way in which historical figures are presented in popular media. Rather than examining the complexities of their lives and legacies, we often see them reduced to one-dimensional caricatures. For example, in the hit musical Hamilton, Alexander Hamilton is portrayed as a brilliant but flawed founding father who ultimately meets a tragic end. However, this romanticized version of history overlooks his role in the creation of the financial system that continues to benefit the wealthy elite today.

Social media has also contributed to the paradox of hating history but loving nostalgia. Platforms like Instagram and

TikTok have given rise to a trend of "vintage" aesthetics that romanticize past eras. This trend includes everything from fashion to music and is often disconnected from the actual social and political issues of the time. For example, the popular trend of 70s fashion overlooks the rise of the conservative movement and the Vietnam War that were major issues of the decade.

Furthermore, the rise of fake news and the spread of misinformation have contributed to a distrust of history and facts. In recent years, we have seen a rise in conspiracy theories reject established historical facts and events, such as the belief the moon landing was faked. This rejection of history in favor of conspiracy theories has contributed to a growing sense of disillusionment with traditional sources of information and knowledge.

The paradox of why Americans hate history, but love nostalgia continues into the 2020s. Despite the wealth of information and digital archives available, many Americans struggle to connect with history on a deeper level. Instead, we see a rise in nostalgia-driven media often romanticizes past eras and overlooks the many social and political issues that plagued them. It is important to recognize the complexities of history and to understand nostalgia is often an incomplete and distorted view of the past.

9 798394 049071